Britannia Pacifics

Gavin Morrison
and Peter Swinger

Ian Allan
PUBLISHING

Contents

Foreword 3

Introduction 4

Acknowledgements and Bibliography 9

Locomotive histories 11

Colour section 66

First published 2003

ISBN 0 7110 2920 2

© Ian Allan Publishing Ltd 2003

Published by Ian Allan Publishing

an imprint of Ian Allan Publishing Ltd, Hersham, Surrey KT12 4RG.
Printed by Ian Allan Printing Ltd, Hersham, Surrey KT12 4RG.

Code: 0310/B

Front cover: Headed by No 70029 *Shooting Star*, the 3.25pm Stourton–Carlisle goods approaches Ribblehead on 18 April 1967; visible on the right are the quarry buildings. The photographer had followed the train by car from Kildwick (south of Skipton), and this was the 14th and final location at which he managed to get a picture! *Gavin Morrison*

Back cover: No 70013 *Oliver Cromwell* bursts out of the tunnel at Lockwood station, Huddersfield, with a railtour on 28 October 1967 — a rare (if not unique) occasion when a 'Britannia' hauled a train between Huddersfield and Penistone. *Gavin Morrison*

Previous page: During the 1950s the 'Golden Arrow', headed by one of the two Stewarts Lane 'Britannias' — Nos 70004 *William Shakespeare* and 70014 *Iron Duke* — was possibly the finest sight on the British Railways network. Both locomotives were kept in immaculate condition, as is apparent from this photograph of No 70004 ready to leave London Victoria. As they normally ran only to Dover and back in a day they accumulated less than 30,000 miles a year — by far the lowest mileage for the class; by contrast, some of the Great Eastern 'Britannias' were covering over 100,000 miles per year in the early 1950s. *Eric Treacy*

Below: An official London Midland Region picture showing No 70000 in BR Brunswick green and named *Britannia*. *Ian Allan Library*

Publisher's Note

When Ian Allan Publishing decided to produce a new book on the subject of the 'Britannia' Pacifics there could only be one candidate to take on the compilation of the book — Peter Swinger. Not only was he an author with whom we had worked well over many years; he had also been involved with the preservation of the first of the class — No 70000 *Britannia* — from the earliest days. Following contracts in early 2002, Peter started work on the book but he was unfortunately never able to complete the project; in the summer of 2002 he was taken seriously ill and was to die suddenly in the September of that year. He had undertaken a considerable amount of work on the development of the book but the project was nowhere near being completed. We are grateful to Gavin Morrison for taking on the challenge of completing the book and grafting his photographic resources on to Peter's researches.

On a personal note, to all who knew him Peter had a wicked sense of humour and seemed to have an endless stream of jokes with which to regale you. Life certainly seems slightly duller without his regular phone calls. This book is intended as a tribute to a class of locomotive; it also serves as a tribute to one of the gentlemen of the railway hobby.

Peter Waller

Foreword

Peter Swinger — Husband, Dad, Friend. He was all these to us, and more. His hobbies and interests were many and varied, but one which stayed with him to his dying day was his beloved *Britannia*.

The love affair started when he rode to school behind various steam locomotives and never ended. I first met *Britannia* when Peter became involved with the East Anglian Locomotive Preservation Society (later to become the Britannia Locomotive Co) and became Editor of its journal, and somehow I found myself as Secretary; he rose to the position of Chairman, and I then became Editor.

Peter's talent for wielding the pen and his love of steam locomotives joined forces and produced many books — of which this is the latest and, sadly, the last.

Peter will be missed by his friends for his knowledge and his company, by the world of steam preservation for his enthusiasm, by his family for the love and fun he brought into our lives and by everyone with whom he came into contact for his terrible jokes and even worse ties!

Kay and Carys Swinger
Stowmarket
May 2003

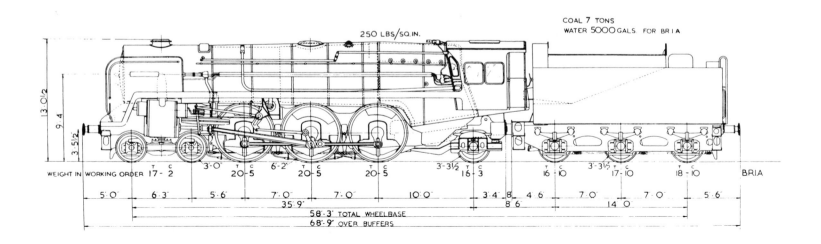

Introduction

They were just 55 in number: their coming transformed the passenger train schedules in East Anglia and, whilst they were not initially welcomed on the Western Region at Old Oak Common, they were eventually accepted, and the men at Canton took them to their hearts. Overall they left their indelible mark on the railways of mainland Great Britain.

British Railways had come into existence as the chimes of midnight rang out on 31 December 1947, taking the vast majority of the railways of England, Scotland and Wales into State ownership; three years and one day later British Railways' first Standard steam locomotive was completed and shortly thereafter moved under its own power for the first time. This was a Class 7MT (mixed-traffic) Pacific with 6ft 2in driving wheels, twin 20 x 28in cylinders, and boiler pressed to 250psi, producing a tractive effort of 32,150lb; the running plate was set high, leaving the driving wheels totally exposed to ease maintenance, in a manner not previously seen on an express passenger locomotive in Britain. The new engines had been designed and built at Crewe under the direction of British Railways' first Chief Mechanical Engineer, Robert Riddles, whose railway career had begun with the London & North Western Railway and continued with the London, Midland & Scottish Railway, where he worked under Sir William Stanier: he had already been responsible for the War Department 2-8-0s and 2-10-0s and the Austerity 0-6-0 tank engines. Under his auspices the Standard steam locomotives would ultimately run to 999 examples, encompassing a number of classes and wheel arrangements.

The remit for the new Standard engines was to produce a series of locomotives which could work throughout the railways of the former 'Big Four', as the new Pacific was intended eventually to replace many 4-6-0 classes then working and coming to the end of their lives (due in no small part to the ravages of war from which the country was still recovering).

Construction of the first Standard Pacific was completed on 2 January 1951; the first recorded outing took place when a test run left Crewe for Carlisle at 12.50 on 11 January 1951, at which time the locomotive was finished in unlined black and simply numbered 70000. The test load was 440 tons of empty stock, including the dynamometer car, and the scheduled time for the non-stop 141.5-mile run was 174min. No 70000 was booked to cover the 90.1 miles from Preston to Carlisle in 145min but actually took only 97min 53sec (an average of just over 50mph) and touched 75mph at Southwaite — a not unimpressive first outing.

Later in the month the engine came down to the capital now resplendent in the British Railways passenger locomotive livery of Brunswick green lined in black and orange — but still unnamed. With due ceremony on 30 January at Marylebone station the Minister of Transport Mr Alfred Barnes named her *Britannia*: because 1951 was Festival of Britain year it was assumed that the name had been chosen for patriotic reasons but many years later when the locomotive had her first rebuild in private ownership Mr Riddles revealed the real reason for the name when he performed the renaming ceremony at Bridgnorth on the Severn Valley Railway. He had chosen the name because the figure of Britannia was incorporated within the heraldic device of the London & North Western Railway.

Left: An official photograph of No 70000 at Crewe Works in the unlined black livery in which it made its first outing, from Crewe to Carlisle, on 11 January 1951. *Ian Allan Library*

Right: A fine study of the front end of No 70027 *Rising Star* at Gloucester Horton Road shed in May 1960. *J. R. Smith*

The initial allocation of 'Britannia' Pacifics was scheduled for East Anglia, where such power had never been known before, express passenger working until then having been in the hands of Gresley and Thompson 4-6-0s, notwithstanding the short-term injection of Pacific power in the form of a loan of some Bulleid Light Pacifics from the Southern Region to ease a somewhat desperate situation. The journey time of the main expresses from Liverpool Street to Ipswich came down to 1hr 15min: the Great Eastern section of the Eastern Region had to wait another 40 years and the coming of electrification to see these times reduced to precisely an hour!

The first eight of the class were allocated to Stratford (30A) and the next seven to Norwich (32A), but Nos 70004 and 70014 were immediately seconded to the Southern Region, where they were allocated to Stewarts Lane (73A) and were on permanent duty working the 'Golden Arrow' — and they never did come to the Eastern Region.

Nos 70015 and 70016 went initially on loan to the London Midland Region before settling at Stratford, whither they were originally intended; then came the first allocations to the Western Region, Nos 70017-20/3 being sent to Old Oak Common (81A) and 70021/2/4 to Plymouth Laira (83D), No 70024 being the final 'Britannia' delivered into traffic in 1951, in October. There was then a lull until September 1952 which saw No 70025 sent to Cardiff

Left: A close-up of the cab and rear bogie of No 70045 *Lord Rowallan* at Liverpool Exchange on 1 September 1967. The cab appears to be in unlined green. *P. Gerald*

Canton (86C), followed by 70026-9 into the November. Nos 70030-3 were sent to Holyhead (6J) in November and December whilst 70034 went to Longsight (9A), and a second batch was sent to East Anglia. Norwich received Nos 70035-7/9/40, whilst 70038/41/2 went to Stratford; Nos 70043 and 70044 were fitted with Westinghouse brake gear and went to the London Midland Region for testing. Holyhead then benefited from the arrival of Nos 70045-9, and the final batch, 70050-4, went to Polmadie, Glasgow (66A), in August and September 1954.

The entire class had been delivered in under three years, and never before had a class of locomotives been so widely distributed in the British Isles — truly they were destined to fulfil their remit of working throughout the network. Sadly the class suffered a ludicrously short working life, some being thrown away when they were barely run in thanks to the Modernisation Plan; the shortest working life was that of No 70050, at just 12 years, and the longest a mere 17 years three months which fell to No 70013 — due in no small part to the fact that it was retained for the end of steam in August 1968.

With the exception of No 70047 the entire class was named, the choice being wide and varied, covering historical figures, poets and gentlemen of a military bent: those allocated to the Western Region, meanwhile, resurrected old Great Western Railway names, while the Scottish allocation was all named after firths.

Above right: Polmadie's No 70054 *Dornoch Firth* prepares to leave Glasgow Central for Edinburgh Princes Street on 15 April 1955. *Gavin Morrison*

Right: No 70004 *William Shakespeare* stands at Crewe North shed on 18 April 1964, at which time it was allocated to Willesden. While its condition does not match that in which it was maintained earlier in its career for 'Golden Arrow' workings, it looks quite clean and has probably not long emerged from works. *Gavin Morrison*

The 'Britannias' were only ever finished in Brunswick green, the one change being in the British Railways tender emblem, but as steam drew to its close the lining was abandoned, and the green was often barely visible beneath the coating of grime which the engines acquired. All were fitted with smoke-deflectors with handrails, to which a modification was made following an accident on the Western Region in which No 70026 was derailed; in the ensuing inquiry the handrails were blamed for unsighting the driver, and they were duly replaced by two styles of hand-holds cut into the smoke-deflectors.

The vast majority of the class were equipped with BR1 tenders which had a coal capacity of seven tons and carried 4,250 gallons of water, but Nos 70025-9 were equipped with BR1A tenders, which had capacity for 5,000 gallons. Nos 70045-54 had the high-sided BR1D variety, which benefited from nine tons' coal capacity and carried 4,725 gallons of water. All had water scoops.

Peter Swinger

Above: An extraordinary picture of No 70014 *Iron Duke* being hauled through Cheadle Heath station by Fowler 2-6-2T No 40067, and still in steam after it had parted company from its tender and the 'Palatine' express on 19 June 1958. *G. Browne*

Left: No 70005, once named *John Milton*, keeps company with Immingham 'B1' No 61406 on the ashpits at Leeds Holbeck shed on 11 April 1965. Like many 'Britannias' by this time, No 70005 is in unlined green. *Gavin Morrison*

Acknowlegements

My thanks as ever to the photographers, especially in the
colour section, who have allowed me to use their material.
It is unfortunate that from 1961 onwards very few were kept
in clean condition, as that is the period when the majority of
colour slides were taken. It is to be hoped that No 70000
Britannia will soon be out and about on the main line again,
for all enthusiasts to enjoy.

Gavin Morrison
Mirfield
June 2003

Bibliography

The Book of the BR Standards by Richard Derry
    (Irwell Press, 1997)
The Power of the BR Standards by G. W. Morrison and
    J. S. Whiteley (Oxford Publishing Co, 1980)
*A Detailed History of British Railways Standard Steam
    Locomotives, Volume One: Background to Standardisation
    and the Pacific Classes* (RCTS, 1994)

A view from the cab of No 70013 *Oliver Cromwell* passing
Accrington at the head of the 'Dalesman No 2' special on
16 June 1968. *Gavin Morrison*

'Britannias' were extremely rare in the North East, but No 70020 *Mercury* was recorded taking coal at West Hartlepool shed after working an excursion from Coventry on 13 March 1965. *I. S. Carr*

70000 *Britannia*

Right: With cab roof painted white, as was customary for Royal engines, No 70000 *Britannia* heads the funeral train for HM King George VI on 11 February 1952. The train had started from Wolferton, being hauled by ex-LNER 'B2' No 61617 *Ford Castle* as far as King's Lynn, where it reversed and *Britannia* took over for the run to King's Cross. *T. Pagano*

Below right: In the immaculate external condition which was the norm for the Stratford 'Britannias', No 70000 *Britannia* pulls out of Liverpool Street at the head of the down 'Norfolkman' during April 1957.
P. Ransome-Wallis

Into traffic	11 January 1951
Named	January 1951
Allocations	Stratford, January 1951
	Norwich, January 1959
	March, September 1961
	Willesden, March 1963
	Crewe North, May 1963
	Crewe South, May 1965
	Newton Heath, March 1966
Withdrawn	May 1966; to preservation

70001 *Lord Hurcomb*

Into traffic	14 February 1951
Named	February 1951
Allocations	Stratford, February 1951
	Norwich, January 1959
	March, September 1959
	Willesden, March 1963
	Aston, December 1963
	Carlisle Kingmoor, October 1964
Withdrawn	August 1966; sold for scrap to Motherwell Machinery & Scrap Co, December 1966

The Carlisle Kingmoor 'Britannias' were cleaned only for special events, sometimes by the shed staff, especially when Carlisle United were doing well in the FA Cup; on other occasions local enthusiasts helped out. No 70001, formerly *Lord Hurcomb*, has obviously not received any such attention for a very long time as it approaches Perth with a down express on 13 August 1965. *Gavin Morrison*

70002 *Geoffrey Chaucer*

Into traffic	6 March 1951
Named	March 1951
Allocations	Stratford, March 1951
	Yarmouth South Town,
	January 1959
	Norwich, January 1959
	March, June 1961
	Carlisle Kingmoor,
	December 1963
Withdrawn	January 1967; sold for scrap
	to G. H. Campbell & Co,
	Airdrie, May 1967

No 70002 *Geoffrey Chaucer* had been allocated to Carlisle Kingmoor for only about two months when this picture was taken of it preparing to leave Bradford Forster Square on the 3.40pm local service to Carlisle on 1 February 1964. This train was regularly worked by 'Britannias' during the last years of steam operation. Later in the year, when heading a freight at Carlisle on 8 August, No 70002 would run into the back of a stationary parcels train but, following repairs, would continue in service until 14 January 1967. *Gavin Morrison*

70003 *John Bunyan*

Into traffic	10 March 1951
Named	March 1951
Allocations	Stratford, March 1951
	Norwich, January 1959
	March, July 1961
	Carlisle Kingmoor, December 1963
Withdrawn	March 1967; sold for scrap to G. H. Campbell & Co, Airdrie, November 1967

A photograph of No 70003 taken at Leeds Holbeck shed on 15 October 1965, by which date the locomotive had lost its *John Bunyan* nameplates, although it is in clean external condition for a Carlisle Kingmoor example. It appears that the locomotive is in plain green livery — there is certainly no lining on the tender, and the small emblem is unusual if not unique for a 'Britannia'. *Gavin Morrison*

70004 *William Shakespeare*

Right: No 70004 *William Shakespeare* was allocated from new to Stratford shed in East London but from April to September 1951 was displayed at the Festival of Britain, following which it settled down to service on the Southern Region from Stewarts Lane. In this superb picture, the locomotive, with all its embellishments, heads the up 'Golden Arrow' past Folkestone Warren on 21 June 1952. *A. C. Cawston*

Below: No 70004 *William Shakespeare*, in its usual immaculate condition, on Stewarts Lane shed. Following transfer from Stewarts Lane in June 1958, the locomotive would be allocated to various LMR sheds. In 1965, after a minor accident, it would become the only 'Britannia' to visit Darlington Works and, indeed, the last steam locomotive to be repaired there before complete closure of the works on 2 April 1966. *Ian Allan Library*

Into traffic	6 March 1951
Named	March 1951
Allocations	Stratford, March 1951
	Stewarts Lane, September 1951
	Kentish Town, June 1958
	Trafford Park, July 1958
	Willesden, December 1960
	Aston, March 1962
	Willesden, April 1962
	Carlisle Canal, May 1963
	Carlisle Kingmoor, June 1963
	Willesden, July 1963
	Crewe North, January 1965
	Stockport Edgeley, May 1965
	Carlisle Kingmoor, June 1967
Withdrawn	December 1967; sold for scrap to T. W. Ward, Inverkeithing, April 1968

70005 *John Milton*

Into traffic	7 April 1951
Named	April 1951
Allocations	Stratford, April 1951
	Rugby Testing Station,
	December 1951
	Stratford, February 1952
	Norwich, January 1959
	March, September 1961
	Willesden, March 1963
	Aston, December 1963
	Carlisle Kingmoor, October 1964
Withdrawn	July 1967; sold for scrap to
	G. H. Campbell & Co, Airdrie,
	January 1968

The shunter at Valley Road Goods, Bradford, has a word with the crew of No 70005 (formerly *John Milton*) just before departure on the 19.40 freight to Carlisle on 13 July 1966.
The locomotive is recorded as running in unlined green livery from June 1964 — although it is impossible to tell from this photograph!
Gavin Morrison

16

70006   *Robert Burns*

Into traffic	12 April 1951
Named	April 1951
Allocations	Stratford, April 1951
	Norwich, May 1951
	Stratford, October 1951
	Norwich, November 1951
	March, December 1961
	Carlisle Kingmoor, December 1963
Withdrawn	May 1967; sold for scrap to J. McWilliam,
	Shettleston, October 1967

A highly atmospheric night shot of No 70006 *Robert Burns* on the ashpits at York shed on 29 August 1963, illustrating well what a dirty place the ashpits used to be. When transferred away from Great Eastern main-line duties from Norwich, in December 1961, this locomotive had achieved the highest mileage for any member of the class — 737,716 miles. *C. P. Walker*

70007 *Coeur-de-Lion*

Into traffic	25 April 1951
Named	April 1951
Allocations	Stratford, April 1951
	Norwich, May 1951
	March, November 1961
	Carlisle Kingmoor, December 1963
Withdrawn	June 1965; scrapped at Crewe Works, July 1965

A brand-new No 70007 *Coeur-de-Lion* makes a superb sight at the head of the 6.35pm Manchester London Road–Crewe stopping train on 26 April 1951 — doubtless a running-in turn before the locomotive was sent to Stratford shed. After spending the majority of its career on the Great Eastern, No 70007 would achieve the dubious distinction of being the only 'Britannia' to be scrapped at a BR works. *T. Lewis*

70008 *Black Prince*

Into traffic	28 April 1951
Named	April 1951
Allocations	Norwich, April 1951
	March, September 1961
	Carlisle Kingmoor, December 1963
Withdrawn	January 1967; sold for scrap to G. H. Campbell & Co, Airdrie, May 1967

Ambling along the Aire Valley in typical latter-day condition, No 70008 (minus its *Black Prince* nameplates) puts up a good exhaust for the photographer as it passes Kirkstall at the head of the 15.25 Stourton Leeds–Carlisle freight on 19 June 1965. *Gavin Morrison*

70009 *Alfred the Great*

Into traffic	4 May 1951
Named	May 1951
Allocations	Norwich, May 1951
	Nine Elms, June 1951
	Norwich, October 1951
	March, September 1961
	Carlisle Kingmoor, December 1963
Withdrawn	January 1967; sold for scrap to J. McWilliam, Shettleston, May 1967

No 70009 *Alfred the Great* went new to Norwich in May 1951 but only stayed one month before being transferred to the Southern Region at Nine Elms, where it stayed for four months. During this period it was used *inter alia* on the 'Bournemouth Belle', being seen here at Bournemouth shed on 7 June 1961 in the company of Adams 'B4' dock tank No 30086. *The Rev G. S. R. Dale*

70010 *Owen Glendower*

Into traffic	5 May 1951
Named	May 1951
Allocations	Norwich, May 1951
	March, December 1961
	Willesden, March 1963
	Crewe North, January 1965
	Crewe South, May 1965
	Carlisle Kingmoor, June 1965
Withdrawn	September 1967; sold for scrap to
	J. McWilliam, Shettleston, April 1968

The 10-coach rugby special from Scotland to Wales appears to have taken its toll on No 70010 *Owen Glendower* after its long climb from Ormside to Ais Gill Summit, as it travels slowly and without much effort towards Shotlock Tunnel on its journey south on 5 February 1967. There were five such specials on this Sunday morning, for which Carlisle Kingmoor turned out four 'Britannias' — Nos 70003, 70010, 70014 and 70039 — and a Brush Type 4 (Class 47) diesel, the last due (it was said) to a failure. No 70010 was the only member of its class to receive a name with a Welsh connection, although by the time this picture was taken the nameplates had been removed and hand-painted names applied, on a green background; the other side featured the Welsh spelling 'Owain Glyndwr'. *Gavin Morrison*

70011 *Hotspur*

Into traffic	14 May 1951
Named	May 1951
Allocations	Norwich, May 1951
	March, September 1961
	Carlisle Kingmoor, December 1963
	Carlisle Upperby, February 1965
	Carlisle Kingmoor, December 1966
Withdrawn	December 1967; sold for scrap to J. McWilliam, Shettleston, April 1968

During its stay at March shed No 70011 *Hotspur* was sent to Doncaster Works for overhaul. Awaiting transfer to the works, it is shown here surrounded by Gresley Pacifics at Doncaster shed on 29 April 1962. *Gavin Morrison*

70012 *John of Gaunt*

Into traffic	21 May 1951
Named	May 1951
Allocations	Norwich, May 1951
	Stratford, October 1958
	Yarmouth South Town, January 1959
	Norwich, January 1959
	March, September 1961
	Willesden, March 1963
	Crewe North, January 1965
	Crewe South, May 1965
	Llandudno Junction, February 1966
	Crewe South, April 1966
	Carlisle Kingmoor, August 1966
Withdrawn	December 1967; sold for scrap to T. W. Ward, Beighton, April 1968

Another member of the class to cover over 700,000 miles whilst working the Great Eastern main line expresses was No 70012 *John of Gaunt*, a Norwich engine when this picture was taken on 5 September 1954 at Stratford. In August 1957 No 70012 would part company from its tender whilst working an express, resulting in the locomotive's running away (one of a number of such instances on GE trains), fortunately without injury to passengers or crew. *R. E. Vincent*

23

70013 *Oliver Cromwell*

Into traffic	30 May 1951
Named	May 1951
Allocations	Norwich, May 1951
	Ipswich, September 1958
	Norwich, January 1959
	March, September 1961
	Carlisle Kingmoor, December 1963
	Carlisle Upperby, February 1965
	Carlisle Kingmoor, December 1966
	Carnforth, January 1968
Withdrawn	August 1968; to preservation at Bressingham

On 16 June 1968 No 70013 *Oliver Cromwell* heads south in fine style with the Railway Correspondence & Travel Society West Riding Branch 'Dalesman No 2' special, one of the many such trains it worked that year. It had taken over the train at Todmorden for the run to Preston, Carnforth and into Skipton, where it was replaced by a BR/Sulzer Type 2 (Class 24) diesel for a visit to the Grassington branch; by this date steam had been banned from the North Eastern Region. No 70013's claim to fame was that, having been the last steam locomotive to be overhauled for British Railways, at Crewe in February 1967, it was chosen to work the last BR steam special, over the Settle & Carlisle, on 11 August 1968. *Gavin Morrison*

70014 *Iron Duke*

Into traffic	2 June 1951
Named	June 1951
Allocations	Norwich, June 1951
	Nine Elms, June 1951
	Stewarts Lane, September 1951
	Kentish Town, June 1958
	Trafford Park, July 1958
	Newton Heath, December 1960
	Willesden, September 1961
	Neasden, September 1961
	Annesley, June 1962
	Willesden, October 1962
	Llandudno Junction, December 1962
	Willesden, May 1963
	Crewe North, January 1965
	Crewe South, May 1965
	Llandudno Junction, February 1966
	Crewe South, April 1966
	Carlisle Kingmoor, August 1966
Withdrawn	December 1967; sold for scrap to
	T. W. Ward, Inverkeithing, March 1968

Above: A fine picture of No 70014 *Iron Duke* leaving Dover Marine on the up 'Golden Arrow' Pullman for London Victoria in April 1956, during the locomotive's glory years at Stewarts Lane shed. Note the ex-LBSCR 'Terrier' tank, No 32636, on the right. *P. Ransome-Wallis*

Left: Its condition contrasting sharply with that shown in the previous picture, No 70014 *Iron Duke* passes Peak Forest at the head of the 5.55pm Manchester Central–London St Pancras following transfer away from Stewarts Lane in 1958. The locomotive would be transferred all over the London Midland Region, including a period at ex-Great Central sheds, before ending its days at Carlisle Kingmoor in August 1966, by which time its BR1 tender had been exchanged for a BR1D. *K. Field*

70015   *Apollo*

During its stay at Stockport Edgeley No 70015 *Apollo* was frequently seen across the Pennines in West Yorkshire and along with the other Edgeley 'Britannias' (Nos 70004/21/6) was kept reasonably clean. With painted nameplate, it is shown piloting Stanier Class 5MT No 45200 of Newton Heath out of the sidings at Neville Hill, Leeds, at the head of the Sunday Heaton–Red Bank (Manchester) van train, which usually exceeded 20 vehicles. Note the handholds on the smoke-deflector, which were fitted by the Western Region in place of handrails after it was suggested that the latter may have blocked the view of the driver in the serious accident involving No 70026 at Milton on 20 November 1955 in which 11 people died. *Gavin Morrison*

Into traffic	12 June 1951	Neasden, September 1961
Named	June 1951	Annesley, June 1962
Allocations	Camden, June 1951	Willesden, October 1962
	Stratford, January 1952	Llandudno Junction, December 1962
	Old Oak Common, September 1953	Crewe North, September 1963
	Cardiff Canton, December 1956	Stockport Edgeley, May 1965
	Trafford Park, July 1958	Carlisle Kingmoor, June 1967
	Newton Heath, December 1960	**Withdrawn**	August 1967; sold for scrap to J. McWilliam,
	Willesden, September 1961		Shettleston, January 1968

70016 *Ariel*

Into traffic	18 June 1951
Named	June 1951
Allocations	Leeds Holbeck, June 1951
	Stratford, March 1952
	Plymouth Laira, August 1953
	Cardiff Canton, December 1956
	Carlisle Canal, September 1961
	Longsight, May 1962
	Crewe North, September 1962
	Llandudno Junction, December 1962
	Holyhead, February 1963
	Aston, May 1963
	Carlisle Kingmoor, October 1964
Withdrawn	August 1967; sold for scrap to J. McWilliam of Shettleston, January 1968

In common with No 70015, No 70016 *Ariel* was intended for the Great Eastern section but was instead sent to the London Midland Region. During its nine months at Leeds Holbeck it worked mainly the expresses over the Settle & Carlisle to Glasgow alongside the rebuilt 'Royal Scots'. By the late 1950s, however, it was based at Cardiff Canton, from which shed it was used on the named expresses to Paddington. It is shown entering Swindon piloting 2-6-2T No 6155 with the up 'Capitals United' on 5 October 1957; evidently, something had gone wrong, as the pair were replaced by Hawksworth 'County' No 1019 *County of Merioneth*. Note the 'Britannia' has had the handrails on its smoke-deflectors replaced by hand-holds. *D. W. T. Bartlett*

70017 Arrow

No 70017 *Arrow* was the first member of the class to be allocated to the Western Region, at Old Oak Common, and is seen on top-link work, passing Thingley Junction with the down 'Merchant Venturer' on 12 April 1952. By all accounts the class was not well received by WR crews except at Cardiff Canton, and records indicate that the WR 'Britannias', other than those at Cardiff, averaged only between 40,000 and 50,000 miles per year; this contrasted with similar locomotives based on the Great Eastern section, which averaged nearly 90,000 miles annually. Following transfer to the LMR, No 70017 would meet a premature end, running into the rear of a freight at Carlisle while heading the 11.45 Glasgow–Morecambe empty-stock train on 3 August 1966.
G. J. Jefferson

Into traffic	23 June 1951		Rugby, October 1962
Named	June 1951		Aston, February 1963
Allocations	Old Oak Common, June 1951		Llandudno Junction, May 1963
	Salisbury, May 1953		Crewe North, September 1963
	Old Oak Common, June 1953		Crewe South, May 1965
	Cardiff Canton, December 1956		Newton Heath, July 1965
	Kentish Town, June 1958		Carlisle Kingmoor, May 1966
	Trafford Park, July 1958	**Withdrawn**	September 1966; sold for scrap
	Willesden, December 1960		to J. Cashmore, Newport,
	Aston, September 1961		February 1967

70018 *Flying Dutchman*

Into traffic	25 June 1951
Named	June 1951
Allocations	Old Oak Common, June 1951
	Cardiff Canton, December 1956
	Carlisle Canal, September 1961
	Longsight, May 1962
	Crewe North, September 1962
	Crewe South, May 1965
	Carlisle Upperby, March 1966
	Carlisle Kingmoor, December 1966
Withdrawn	December 1966; sold for scrap to Motherwell Machinery & Scrap Co, May 1967

After 10 years' service on the Western Region, No 70018 *Flying Dutchman* moved to Carlisle Canal and during its time on the LMR would be allocated to all three sheds at Carlisle. However, this fine picture shows the locomotive surrounded by a wide variety of wagons together with an Ivatt 2-6-2T at Crewe North shed, probably when based there in the early 1960s. *J. R. Carter*

70019 *Lightning*

Into traffic	30 June 1951
Named	June 1951
Allocations	Newton Abbot, June 1951
	Plymouth Laira, September 1951
	Cardiff Canton, December 1956
	Carlisle Kingmoor, September 1961
	Longsight, June 1962
	Crewe North, September 1962
	Aston, May 1963
	Crewe North, September 1963
	Crewe South, May 1965
	Carlisle Upperby, July 1965
Withdrawn	March 1966; sold for scrap to West of Scotland Shipbreaking Co, Troon, May 1966

No 70019 *Lightning* was the only 'Britannia' to be allocated new to Newton Abbot (although No 70022 *Tornado* would spend over four years at the shed), and it is interesting to note that, unlike their colleagues at Cardiff Canton, the WR crews in the South West did not generally take to the new Standards. Transferred to the Welsh capital in 1956, No 70019 is pictured waiting to take over an up express at Cardiff General on 3 August 1957; its superb external condition gives an idea of how the locomotive was appreciated at its new home.
J. Hodge

70020 *Mercury*

Into traffic	31 July 1951
Named	July 1951
Allocations	Old Oak Common, July 1951
	Cardiff Canton, December 1956
	Carlisle Kingmoor, September 1961
	Longsight, June 1962
	Crewe North, September 1962
	Carlisle Canal, January 1963
	Willesden, May 1963
	Crewe North, January 1965
	Crewe South, May 1965
	Carlisle Upperby, July 1965
	Carlisle Kingmoor, December 1966
Withdrawn	January 1967; sold for scrap to
	J. McWilliam, Shettleston, May 1967

Right: No 70020 *Mercury* was only a month old when this fine picture was taken of it heading the down 'Merchant Venturer' past Langley Crossing, Chippenham, on 29 August 1951. Note the handrails and the bracket for the train reporting number, although the latter is not in use. *G. J. Jefferson*

Right: In later life, whilst allocated to Willesden, *Mercury* was selected to work the Southern Counties Touring Society's 'South West Ramblers' special. Looking well-cleaned, it is seen away from its normal haunts, emerging from Salisbury Tunnel on the approach to the station on 8 March 1964. This was another member of the class to be allocated to all the three Carlisle sheds during its career, which would draw to a close at Kingmoor in December 1966. *Hugh Ballantyne*

31

70021 *Morning Star*

Into traffic	3 August 1951
Named	August 1951
Allocations	Plymouth Laira, August 1951
	Cardiff Canton, January 1957
	Trafford Park, July 1958
	Willesden, February 1961
	Aston, March 1962
	Willesden, March 1962
	Crewe North, January 1965
	Crewe South, May 1965
	Newton Heath, July 1965
	Stockport Edgeley, May 1966
	Carlisle Kingmoor, June 1967
Withdrawn	December 1967; sold for scrap to
	T. W. Ward, Inverkeithing, April 1968

No 70021 *Morning Star* was one of a number of 'Britannias' to be allocated new to Plymouth Laira, from which shed they worked across the Saltash Bridge into Cornwall, becoming the first Pacifics and the largest locomotives regularly to work in the Duchy. However, like its classmates, No 70021 would end its career far away from Cornwall; recorded during its last six months of service, from Carlisle Kingmoor, it presents a sad sight at the head of an up freight passing Carnforth. The now famous coaling tower at Steamtown can be seen in the distance. *Ian Allan Library*

70022 *Tornado*

Into traffic	16 August 1951
Named	August 1951
Allocations	Plymouth Laira, August 1951
	Newton Abbot, April 1952
	Cardiff Canton, December 1956
	Carlisle Kingmoor, September 1961
	Longsight, June 1962
	Aston, September 1962
	Rugby, October 1962
	Aston, February 1963
	Carlisle Kingmoor, October 1964
	Carlisle Upperby, November 1964
	Carlisle Kingmoor, December 1966
Withdrawn	December 1967; sold for scrap to T. W. Ward, Inverkeithing, April 1968

When less than one month old, No 70022 *Tornado* makes a fine sight leaving Bristol Temple Meads at the head of the 11.55 Manchester London Road–Plymouth at 6.5pm on 15 September 1951. The locomotive had probably taken over at Shrewsbury, as this train travelled via the North & West route. By today's standards six hours from Manchester to Bristol seems a long time! *Ian Allan Library*

70023 *Venus*

Into traffic	21 August 1951		Aston, February 1963
Named	August 1951		Crewe North, September 1963
Allocations	Old Oak Common, August 1951		Holyhead, September 1964
	Salisbury, May 1953		Crewe North, February 1965
	Old Oak Common, June 1953		Crewe South, May 1965
	Cardiff Canton, February 1957		Llandudno Junction, February 1966
	Carlisle Kingmoor, September 1961		Crewe South, April 1966
	Longsight, June 1962		Carlisle Kingmoor, September 1966
	Aston, September 1962	**Withdrawn**	December 1967; sold for scrap to
	Rugby, October 1962		T. W. Ward, Beighton, March 1968

No 70023 *Venus* began its career on the Western Region, but on 20 January 1952, along with No 70020 *Mercury,* it was tested with a dynamometer on the Midland main line, hauling a 100-wagon mineral train, weighing 1,200 tons, between Toton and Brent. The train is shown passing Bedford, apparently travelling very fast for a Class C fitted freight. *P. J. Lynch*

70024 *Vulcan*

No 70024 *Vulcan* was the last 'Britannia' to be allocated new to the West Country. In May 1953, when all the 'Merchant Navys' were temporarily withdrawn, it was one of four (the others being Nos 70023/8/9) loaned to the Southern Region for working Waterloo–Exeter trains, and contemporary articles suggest the SR put up some good performances with them, easily maintaining 'Merchant Navy' schedules. Later in life No 70024 was transferred to the London Midland Region; here, looking unusually clean for a Kingmoor locomotive, it waits its turn in the loop behind two BR/Sulzer Type 2 diesels near Leeds Holbeck shed with a freight from Leeds (Stourton) to Carlisle on 1 May 1967. *Gavin Morrison*

Into traffic	6 October 1951	Crewe North, November 1963
Named	October 1951	Holyhead, September 1964
Allocations	Plymouth Laira, October 1951	Crewe North, February 1965
	Exmouth Junction, May 1953	Crewe South, May 1965
	Plymouth Laira, June 1953	Llandudno Junction, February 1966
	Cardiff Canton, December 1956	Crewe South, April 1966
	Aston, September 1961	Carlisle Upperby, August 1966
	Rugby, October 1962	Carlisle Kingmoor, December 1966
	Aston, February 1963	**Withdrawn** December 1967; sold for scrap to
	Willesden, April 1963	T. W. Ward, Killamarsh, April 1968

70025 *Western Star*

Into traffic	13 September 1952
Named	September 1952
Allocations	Cardiff Canton, September 1952
	Rugby Testing Station, September 1952
	Cardiff Canton, May 1953
	Aston, September 1961
	Crewe North, May 1963
	Crewe South, May 1965
	Llandudno Junction, February 1966
	Crewe South, April 1966
	Carlisle Kingmoor, September 1966
Withdrawn	December 1967; sold for scrap to
	G. H. Campbell & Co, Airdrie,
	January 1968

No 70025 *Western Star* was the first of a batch of five (70025-9) allocated new to Cardiff Canton. Each had a BR1A tender, giving an extra 750 gallons of water capacity (5,000 gallons) over the BR1. The Cardiff crews took a liking to the new locomotives and they were kept in tip-top condition. In the mid-1950s these five locomotives were achieving annual mileages of nearly 70,000, whereas the Old Oak Common and West Country engines managed only around 45,000; the Great Eastern locomotives, meanwhile, were in the upper 70,000s and some well into the 80,000s, or even higher.

By the time this photograph was taken, on 16 April 1967, No 70025 was working out its last months of service from Carlisle Kingmoor and is seen heading a rugby football overnight special from Cardiff back to Scotland. Few of the passengers are likely to have been awake as the train passed Selside, on the Settle & Carlisle, around 7.30am. *Gavin Morrison*

70030   *William Wordsworth*

Into traffic	19 November 1952
Named	November 1952
Allocations	Holyhead, November 1952
	Longsight, December 1952
	Leeds Holbeck, January 1953
	Longsight, February 1953
	Dover, May 1953
	Longsight, June 1953
	Norwich, July 1953
	Yarmouth South Town, October 1958
	Norwich, January 1959
	March, June 1961
	Crewe North, July 1963
	Crewe South, May 1965
	Carlisle Upperby, July 1965
Withdrawn	June 1966; sold for scrap to
	T. W. Ward Ltd, Beighton,
	August 1966

No 70030 *William Wordsworth* simmers gently in the evening light at Carnforth shed on 26 August 1964. This locomotive had an unusual start to its career, being transferred no fewer than six times in its first nine months, its wanderings including a month at Dover covering for the temporary withdrawal of the 'Merchant Navys'. It would end its days at Carlisle Upperby, being one of the few 'Britannias' not withdrawn from Kingmoor. *Gavin Morrison*

70031 *Byron*

Into traffic	29 November 1952
Named	November 1952
Allocations	Holyhead, November 1952
	Longsight, January 1953
	Trafford Park, April 1960
	Longsight, September 1960
	Aston, September 1961
	Willesden, April 1963
	Crewe North, January 1965
	Crewe South, May 1965
	Carlisle Upperby, July 1965
	Carlisle Kingmoor, December 1966
Withdrawn	November 1967; sold for scrap to J. McWilliam, Shettleston, April 1968

Nos 70030-3 all went new to Holyhead, but their stay only lasted a few weeks, as the water capacity of the BR1 tender was insufficient for working the Euston services. No 70031 *Byron* put in seven years working from Longsight alongside the rebuilt 'Scots' on the main Euston diagrams until the English Electric Type 4 (Class 40) diesels took over. The locomotive is pictured south of Nuneaton at the head of the 2.45pm Euston–Manchester London Road on 12 April 1958. *M. Mensing*

70032 *Tennyson*

Into traffic	10 December 1952
Named	17 March 1953
Allocations	Holyhead, December 1952
	Longsight, January 1953
	Trafford Park, February 1960
	Willesden, January 1961
	Carlisle Kingmoor, October 1964
	Carlisle Upperby, November 1964
	Carlisle Kingmoor, December 1966
Withdrawn	September 1967; sold for scrap to
	J. McWilliam, Shettleston,
	January 1968

Right: During 1953, the first year of seven spent working from Longsight shed, No 70032 *Tennyson* arrives at Euston at the head of the up 'Mancunian', complete with headboard. *G. Rixon*

Below right: After seven years working the Euston services, *Tennyson* moved across Manchester to work the London services to St Pancras. Presumably cleaners at Trafford Park were at a premium in 1960, judging from this picture of the locomotive preparing to leave Leeds City with the up 'Thames–Clyde Express' on 7 August 1960. However, such workings were soon taken over by BR/Sulzer Type 4 'Peak' (Class 45) diesels, the 'Britannias' thus displaced being reallocated around the London Midland Region. *Gavin Morrison*

70033 *Charles Dickens*

Into traffic	13 December 1952
Named	December 1952
Allocations	Holyhead, December 1952
	Longsight, January 1953
	Trafford Park, February 1960
	Willesden, February 1961
	Llandudno Junction, December 1962
	Holyhead, March 1963
	Willesden, May 1963
	Crewe North, September 1963
	Crewe South, May 1965
	Carlisle Kingmoor, June 1965
Withdrawn	July 1967; sold for scrap to G. H. Campbell & Co, Airdrie, November 1967

Above left: A fine picture of No 70033 *Charles Dickens* working the up 'Mancunian' (12 coaches) near Chelford on 28 March 1957. Like No 70032, when new this locomotive spent only a month at Holyhead before being allocated to Longsight in January 1953 and would be transferred to Trafford Park in February 1960. *T. Lewis*

Left: When this picture was taken on 6 August 1963 *Charles Dickens* had been borrowed from Willesden to work the 2.38pm Marylebone–Nottingham semi-fast, seen entering Ashby Magna. Passenger services would be withdrawn from this stretch of the Great Central main line on 5 May 1969. *G. D. King*

70038 *Robin Hood*

Into traffic	29 January 1953
Named	January 1953
Allocations	Stratford, January 1953
	Norwich, January 1959
	March, November 1960
	Immingham, October 1961
	Carlisle Upperby, December 1963
	Carlisle Kingmoor, January 1964
Withdrawn	August 1967; sold for scrap to J. McWilliam, Shettleston, January 1968

No 70038 *Robin Hood* was selected to haul a Stephenson Locomotive Society special across the Pennines on the Standedge route to York on 2 July 1967. In this view it has just climbed the short, steep gradient from Whitehall Junction, Leeds, to Copley Hill before heading towards Farnley. The locomotive was turned out in good external condition with a painted name, although, cabsides apart, it appears to be in unlined green. *Gavin Morrison*

70039 *Sir Christopher Wren*

Into traffic	9 February 1953
Named	February 1953
Allocations	Norwich, February 1953
	Stratford, May 1953
	Norwich, January 1959
	Immingham, December 1960
	Carlisle Upperby, December 1963
	Carlisle Kingmoor, February 1964
Withdrawn	September 1967; sold for scrap to J. McWilliam, Shettleston, January 1968

With Wild Boar fell shrouded in mist, No 70039, bereft of its *Sir Christopher Wren* nameplates, passes Ais Gill Summit in fine style with one of the five rugby supporters' specials returning from Edinburgh to Wales on the morning of Sunday 5 February 1967. *Gavin Morrison*

70054 *Dornoch Firth*

Into traffic	13 September 1954
Named	February 1955
Allocations	Polmadie, September 1954
	Leeds Holbeck, October 1958
	Crewe North, August 1962
	Willesden, March 1964
	Crewe North, July 1964
	Crewe South, May 1965
	Banbury, September 1965
	Carlisle Kingmoor, January 1966
Withdrawn	November 1966; sold for scrap to Motherwell Machinery & Scrap Co, May 1967

No 70054, later named *Dornoch Firth*, was the last of the class to be built, at a cost of £23,987 — £3,873 more than *Britannia* had cost, less than four years earlier. Nos 70053 and 70054 left Polmadie earlier than Nos 70050-2 and were transferred to Leeds Holbeck for working the Scottish expresses over the Settle & Carlisle, which resulted in two of the long-standing rebuilt 'Scots' on Holbeck's allocation (Nos 46103 and 46133) moving to Kentish Town. Here No 70054, still with the old 'lion-and-wheel' emblem on its tender, crosses the famous Ribblehead Viaduct — 440yd long and 104ft high — at the head of the down 'Thames–Clyde Express' on 16 May 1959. *Gavin Morrison*

Above: In typical external condition for a Carlisle Kingmoor locomotive, No 70036, formerly *Boadicea*, is seen just north of Stonehaven at the head of a freight on 29 June 1966. *D. Marriott*

Right: No 70008 *Black Prince* pulls away from Perth and prepares to enter Moncrieff Tunnel with an up express on 28 August 1965. The site of the former Perth shed (63A) can just be seen through the bridge in the background. *D. Marriott*

Left: No 70045 *Lord Rowallan* storms up Beattock Bank past Greskine with a heavy Manchester Victoria–Glasgow Central express on 4 June 1960; the banking locomotive — a Fairburn 2-6-4T — is out of sight. *Gavin Morrison*

Above: Complete with its large, two-line nameplate, No 70048 *The Territorial Army 1908-1958* basks in the evening sunshine at Carlisle Upperby shed on 28 November 1964. *Gavin Morrison*

Left: Returning Wales supporters from a rugby match at Murrayfield, No 70010 *Owen Glendower* storms through Kirkby Stephen and heads for the summit of Ais Gill on the morning of Sunday 5 February 1967. *Gavin Morrison*

Above: Having just left Birkett Tunnel, No 70002 *Geoffrey Chaucer* continues its climb to Ais Gill with a relief to the up 'Thames–Clyde Express' on 4 July 1964. *Gavin Morrison*

Above: No 70006 *Robert Burns* puts on a fine exhaust in the winter sunshine of 18 January 1964 as it approaches Dent at the head of a down freight for Carlisle. *Gavin Morrison*

Right: Train IT57, the famous 'Fifteen Guinea Special', approaches Ribblehead station hauled by No 70013 *Oliver Cromwell* on 11 August 1968 — the last day of non-preserved British Rail steam operation. The train ran from Liverpool to Carlisle via the Settle & Carlisle and returned behind Class 5MTs Nos 44781 and 44871. Considering the cost of the trip, one would have thought BR could at least have made a nameplate for the locomotive! *Gavin Morrison*

Above: During 1965, 1966 and 1967 the 15.25 Bradford Forster Square–Carlisle stopper — not exactly a heavy train — was regularly hauled by a 'Britannia'. On 12 May 1967 No 70037 *Hereward the Wake* passes Hirst Wood, between Shipley and Bingley, on its journey north. *Gavin Morrison*

Right: In the mid-1960s the 19.40 Bradford (Valley Road Goods)–Carlisle freight was a regular working for a Kingmoor 'Britannia'. No 70003 *John Bunyan* prepares to leave the yard on 29 June 1966. *Gavin Morrison*

Above: Seen between duties outside Manningham shed, Bradford, on 21 March 1967, No 70034 *Thomas Hardy* has had its original BR1 tender replaced by a BR1D type. This site is now occupied by industrial units. *Gavin Morrison*

Right: No 70004 *William Shakespeare* passes through Rodley Cutting, near Leeds, with the 12.55 Stourton– Carlisle freight on 21 August 1967. The locomotive's condition is in stark contrast to that in which it was maintained by Stewarts Lane for working the 'Golden Arrow' in the 1950s. *Gavin Morrison*

Left: On 9 March 1961 Leeds Holbeck-allocated No 70044 *Earl Haig* passes Wortley Junction, Leeds, as it gets into its stride at the head of the down 'Waverley', which it would work as far as Carlisle. *Gavin Morrison*

Above: No 70003 *John Bunyan* on Holbeck shed, being prepared for the 12.55 freight from Stourton to Carlisle, on 15 October 1965. Note that the locomotive is in unlined green livery; also the small emblem on the tender. *Gavin Morrison*

Left: In terrible external condition, Holbeck's No 70044 *Earl Haig* prepares to leave its home shed and back down to Leeds City to work the 'Thames-Clyde Express' to Carlisle on 13 September 1960. *Gavin Morrison*

Below left: No 70035 *Rudyard Kipling* was a very unusual visitor to Leeds Neville Hill shed on 17 October 1964. The time was not 5.45, as suggested by the clock on the water tower, but 1pm. *Gavin Morrison*

Right: A very rare (and possibly the only) visit of a 'Britannia' to the Huddersfield–Penistone line on a passenger train: No 70013 *Oliver Cromwell* is shown very near to Penistone (just before the viaduct) at the head of a special on 28 October 1967. *Gavin Morrison*

Above: A well-cleaned No 70038 *Robin Hood* passes Neville Hill, Leeds, prior to entering Marsh Lane Cutting with a Stephenson Locomotive Society special from York on 2 July 1967. *Gavin Morrison*

Right: Another view of the same SLS special, at Bradley Junction (east of Huddersfield); in 1967 there were four tracks, but today only the two on the right survive. Note that No 70038's tender is in unlined green, while the locomotive itself has retained its lining on the cabside. *Gavin Morrison*

Above: On 7 May 1966 the Heaton–Red Bank (Manchester) empty newspaper-van train — which regularly consisted of 20-25 vans — was headed by No 70011 *Hotspur* and Stanier Class 5MT No 44947, seen passing Cooper Bridge, between Mirfield and Brighouse. The lines on the right have now been lifted. *Gavin Morrison*

Right: Another view of the Heaton–Red Bank vans, this time passing Brighouse behind No 70018 *Flying Dutchman* and Class B1 4-6-0 No 61030 *Nyala* on 28 May 1966. This train was famous for its wide variety of motive power and was often double-headed north of York by Eastern Region Pacifics. *Gavin Morrison*

Immingham shed had an allocation of 'Britannias' for working express freight and passenger trains to/from Grimsby, but occasionally they were used on excursions. Here, on 8 September 1963, No 70039 *Sir Christopher Wren* passes Sowerby Bridge, on the Calder Valley main line, at the head of a special to Blackpool Illuminations. *Gavin Morrison*

On 28 June 1961, during its nine-month stay at Newton Heath shed, No 70015
Apollo was used on a passenger working via the Calder Valley route to
Manchester — rare for a 'Britannia'. The train is seen between Luddendenfoot
and Mytholmroyd. *Gavin Morrison*

Left: No 70051 *Firth of Forth* approaches Shap Summit at the head of a heavy Manchester Victoria–Glasgow Central express on 24 August 1963. *Gavin Morrison*

Above: Another picture of No 70051 *Firth of Forth*, here putting up a fine exhaust as it passes Fulwood, north of Preston, with the same train on 24 August 1963. *D. Marriott*

Left: In fine weather, No 70010 *Owen Glendower* passes Farrington, south of Preston, with a down express on the afternoon of 19 May 1964. *D. Marriott*

Above: No 70032 *Tennyson* blows off steam approaching Leyland at the head of a train for Manchester Victoria on 11 September 1965. *D. Marriott*

Left: Pictured at the head of a Summer Saturday extra on the North Wales Coast main line on 22 June 1963, No 70023 *Venus* has obviously been given a clean by Aston shed. The train is passing the site of Mochdre & Pabo station, which closed to passenger traffic on 5 January 1931. This section of track now finds itself hard up against the A55 dual carriageway. *Gavin Morrison*

Below: No 70019 *Lightning* passes West Shore, between Llandudno and Deganwy, with a Sunday-afternoon express to Birmingham New Street on 31 March 1963. *Gavin Morrison*

Above: No 70000 *Britannia* inside Crewe Works after what was probably its last visit for overhaul on 18 April 1964, when allocated to Crewe North shed. *Gavin Morrison*

Right: Prior to the introduction of the Class 45 'Peaks' on the Scottish expresses north of Leeds, the Holbeck 'Britannias' seldom worked south of the city. In terrible condition externally, No 70053 *Moray Firth* passes Dore & Totley at the head of the down 'Thames–Clyde Express' on 9 July 1960. *D. Marriott*

Above: No 70013 *Oliver Cromwell* blows off steam as it passes Hasland, near Chesterfield, with a special for Norwich on 9 June 1968. *Gavin Morrison*

Right: No 70046 *Anzac* arrives at Birmingham New Street's Platform 6 with empty stock for the 1.40pm to Liverpool Lime Street and Manchester Piccadilly on 25 March 1961. *M. Mensing*

Left: No 70036 *Boadicea* pauses at Retford at the head of a Sheffield Victoria–Cleethorpes on 22 June 1963, at which date the locomotive was allocated to Immingham shed. *D. Marriott*

Above: Immingham-allocated No 70040 *Clive of India* rushes along the East Coast main line near Potters Bar at the head of a King's Cross–Cleethorpes express on 13 May 1961. *D. Marriott*

Above: In dirty condition, No 70049 *Solway Firth* stands at Neasden shed in March 1962, during its brief (nine-month) period of allocation there. *G. Rixon*

Right: Pictured at its then home shed of Willesden, No 70021 *Morning Star* looks as if it has just returned from a general overhaul in May 1963. *G. Rixon*

Above: Minus its *Moray Firth* nameplates and in terrible condition externally, No 70053 heads the 10.05 Kingswear–Wolverhampton past the remains of Winchcombe station, on the Cheltenham–Stratford-upon-Avon line, on 31 July 1965. *M. Mensing*

Right: No 70053 rounds the curve between Hatton West and Hatton North junctions, south of Birmingham, with the Saturdays-only 10.05 Kingswear–Wolverhampton on 21 August 1965. *M. Mensing*

Left: No 70036 *Boadicea* awaits attention on the ashpits at Stratford shed on 13 September 1958 after working the up 'Hook Continental', as is apparent from the headboard. *Gavin Morrison*

Above: The two 'express' white headcode discs stand out against a dirty No 70037 *Hereward the Wake* as it prepares to leave Liverpool Street with an express for East Anglia in the late 1950s. *R. C. Riley collection*

Left: In the usual immaculate Cardiff Canton condition, No 70024 *Vulcan* races through Sonning Cutting at the head of the up 'Red Dragon' on 13 May 1961. Four months later the locomotive would be transferred to the LMR and would likely never be seen as clean again. *D. Marriott*

Right: No 70016 *Ariel* climbs away from Severn Tunnel and approaches Pilning with the 7.30am from Pembroke Dock (7.50 from Fishguard) to Paddington on 28 September 1959. *M. Mensing*

Right: On 22 May 1961, after working the up 'Red Dragon' in the morning, No 70024 *Vulcan* returned to Cardiff in the afternoon on the down 'Capitals United Express', seen just west of Twyford. *D. Marriott*

Above: Not in the external condition normally associated with Cardiff Canton 'Britannias', No 70027 *Rising Star* passes through Sonning Cutting with an express for Paddington in the summer of 1961. The following September, the locomotive would move away from the Western Region to Aston shed on the London Midland. *D. Marriott*

Right: No 70018 *Flying Dutchman* passes Old Oak Common at the head of the 3.45pm Paddington–Fishguard on 29 August 1959. *R. C. Riley*

Left: The 'Golden Arrow' Pullman in all its glory, passing through the London suburb of Herne Hill on 20 October 1957 behind No 70014 *Iron Duke*, which was usually the standby locomotive for this duty. *R. C. Riley*

Right: Probably the first time a Stockport Edgeley-allocated locomotive visited Salisbury shed: No 70004 is seen prior to use on part of the Locomotive Club of Great Britain's 'A2' Commemorative Rail Tour' special from Waterloo to Exeter on 14 August 1966. The locomotive is in unlined green except for the cabside and tender, which have been treated to black lining but no orange; this gave the locomotive a rather odd appearance and is believed to have been applied by the shed staff at Edgeley. *Hugh Ballantyne*